Our Emotions and Behaviour

I Don't Want to Wait!

Written by Sue Graves

Illustrated by
Emanuela Carletti and
Desideria Guicciardini

Maisy was **never patient.**
She hated waiting for her birthday even
when it was ages away!

At school, she **wouldn't wait patiently** to see Miss Chen even though there were others before her in the line.

5

Maisy hated waiting for her turn to speak in News Time. She always interrupted others when they were speaking. Miss Chen said it was **rude to interrupt.**

When Maisy got impatient, she got cross. She **shouted and yelled** over other people so no one could hear what they were saying.

One day, Miss Chen said everyone was going to make animal masks. She said all the children should **paint them carefully.** She said they would need to wait patiently for the paint to dry.

8

But Maisy didn't wait patiently. She **didn't wait for the paint to dry** at all. The paint dripped all over her. Miss Chen was cross.

That afternoon after school, Raffi came to play. He brought his new game. He told Maisy that they had to **take turns** to roll the dice.

But Maisy didn't want to wait for her turn. She **snatched the dice** from Raffi. Raffi was upset.

That Saturday, Maisy's big sister, Lola, was coming to stay. Maisy loved Lola – she was really good fun. But Lola phoned to say her bus **was late**.

Mum said Maisy would have to **wait patiently** for her sister to arrive. Maisy scowled crossly and tapped her foot.

Later that afternoon, Lola arrived.
Maisy wanted to play shops with her
immediately. But Lola said she wanted
to have a chat with Mum first. She said
she'd play shops after that.

Maisy got very cross.
She **stamped upstairs** to
her bedroom and **slammed the
door hard**.

After a while, Maisy **calmed down**.
She wished she hadn't stamped her feet.
She wished she hadn't slammed her
door.

She went to find Lola.

Maisy told her sister she was sorry. Lola said everyone feels impatient sometimes. She told Maisy she felt impatient when her bus was late, so she took **a deep breath** and thought about other things. She said that made her feel better.

Maisy said that if she felt impatient again, maybe she could take a deep breath and **think about other things**, too.

The next day, Lola and Maisy went to the park. Maisy ran to the slide, but Raffi had got there first. He was going very, very slowly down the slide.

Maisy took **a deep breath**.
She looked for shapes in the clouds.
She waited patiently for her turn.

Then Lola said it was time for ice creams.
But the ice-cream man was very busy, so
Maisy had to **wait patiently**
at the back of the line. She counted all
the different flavours.

She even made up some of her own!

At last, it was Maisy's turn. The man said she had waited very patiently. He gave her an extra dollop of ice cream for being so patient. Maisy said it was so

much nicer to be patient!

Can you tell the story of what happened when George and his dad baked a cake?

How do you think George felt when his cake wasn't ready? How did he feel at the end?

A note about sharing this book

The *Our Emotions and Behaviour* series has been developed to provide a starting point for further discussion on children's feelings and behaviour, both in relation to themselves and to other people.

I Don't Want to Wait!
This book looks at the importance of being patient and understanding that not everything can happen immediately – and as it turns out, realising that some things are worth waiting for.

The book aims to encourage children to have a developing awareness of behavioural expectations in different settings. It also invites children to begin to consider the consequences of their words and actions for themselves and others.

Storyboard puzzle
The wordless storyboard on pages 26 and 27 provides an opportunity for speaking and listening. Children are encouraged to tell the story illustrated in the panels: George and his dad are baking a cake, and George doesn't want to wait for it to bake. He asks his dad to take the cake out of the oven too early and the cake collapses. On the next attempt, George is more patient and the cake comes out perfectly.

How to use the book
The book is designed for adults to share with either an individual child, or a group of children, and as a starting point for discussion.

The book also provides visual support and repeated words and phrases to build confidence in children who are starting to read on their own.

Before reading the story
Choose a time to read when you and the children are relaxed and have time to share the story.

Spend time looking at the illustrations and talk about what the book may be about before reading it together.

After reading, talk about the book with the children:

- What was the book about? Have the children ever been impatient for an exciting event to happen? Examples might be a birthday or a special party. How did they feel? Did it seem to them that time passed slowly when they especially wanted something to happen?

- Have they ever rushed a task and perhaps spoilt the outcome through rushing and being impatient? Invite the children to share their experiences with the others.

- As a group talk about why it is important to be patient when, for example, playing a game. Why can being impatient spoil a game for others? Extend this by talking about the importance of waiting your turn in class, either to speak in group time or to ask for the teacher's attention. Encourage the children to take turns to speak and to listen politely while others are talking.

- Look at the storyboard puzzle and talk about what is happening in the story. Invite children to play out the storyboard. Discuss performances afterwards as a group.

- Talk about being patient in school generally. Explain that being part of a school community requires levels of patience. The teacher may be busy helping another child before they can help you.

- Waiting for your turn in a game requires patience for the game to be played successfully.

- Look at the end of the story together and talk about the way Maisy takes her mind off waiting by thinking about other things.

- Ask the children to write or draw things they could think about while they have to wait for something. Make a display of their work.

29

To Isabelle, William A, George, William G, Max, Emily,
Leo, Caspar, Felix and Phoebe – S.G.

Franklin Watts
First published in Great Britain in 2019 by The Watts Publishing Group

ISBN (hardback) 978 1 4451 6552 3
ISBN (paperback) 978 1 4451 6553 0

Editor: Jackie Hamley
Designer: Peter Scoulding

Printed in China

FSC
www.fsc.org
MIX
Paper from
responsible sources
FSC® C104740

Franklin Watts
An imprint of
Hachette Children's Group
Part of The Watts Publishing Group
Carmelite House
50 Victoria Embankment
London EC4Y 0DZ

An Hachette UK Company
www.hachette.co.uk

www.franklinwatts.co.uk